CW00394686

PYGMY GC

A Comprehensive Guide To Raising, Caring For, And Understanding These Adorable Miniature Companions

Remy Harrington

Table of Contents

CHAPTER ONE 3

    INTRODUCTION TO PYGMY GOATS 3

    CHOOSING AND CARING ON PYGMY GOATS 8

CHAPTER TWO 15

    BREEDING AND REPRODUCTION 15

    PYGMY GOAT BEHAVIOR AND SOCIAL DESIGN 20

CHAPTER THREE 25

    TRAINING AND ADVANCEMENT FOR PYGMY GOATS 25

    PYGMY GOAT HEALTH AND COMMON DISEASES 29

CHAPTER FOUR 35

    PREVENTIVE HEALTH MEASURES 35

    RECOGNIZING INDICATIONS OF SICKNESS 40

CHAPTER FIVE.. 45

    PYGMY GOATS IN SUSTAINABLE AGRICULTURE 45

    PYGMY GOAT BREEDING FOR BEIGNNERS...................... 50

CHAPTER SIX... 56

    PYGMY GOATS AS PETS: CONTEMPLATIONS AND CARE 56

    PYGMY GOAT MILK AND DAIRY CREATION 61

CHAPTER SEVEN 66

    PYGMY GOAT GENETICS AND COLORS VARIATIATIONS 66

    PYGMY GOAT CARE IN VARIOUS ENVIRONMENTS.............. 70

    CONCLUSION 75

THE END 79

CHAPTER ONE

INTRODUCTION TO PYGMY GOATS

Pygmy goats are a little and strong type of homegrown goat that began in West Africa. They are known for their smaller size, amicable disposition, and adaptability, which have made them famous as pets, companions, and even show creatures. Here is an introduction to Pygmy goats:

Origin and History: Pygmy goats, deductively known as Capra aegagrus hircus, were at first found in the Cameroon Valley of West Africa. They were imported to the United States during the mid-20th century for show purposes and immediately gained ubiquity because of their beguiling appearance and manageable size.

Physical Characteristics: Pygmy goats are outstandingly more modest than most other goat breeds, ranging around 16 to 23 inches tall at the shoulder. Their weight ranges between 40 to 85 pounds, with males (bucks) being bigger than females (does). They have a stocky and solid form, with a short, wide head and a particular facial profile. Their coats arrive in different tones and patterns, including strong, agouti, and different combinations.

Personality and Behavior: Pygmy goats are prestigious for their well disposed and friendly nature. They are interested, playful, and for the most part coexist well with people, making them reasonable mates and pets. Because of their little size, they are frequently preferred by families with youngsters or people with restricted space. Pygmy goats have a characteristic tendency to investigate their environmental elements and engage in playful jokes, making them great to watch and connect with.

Housing and Care: Giving suitable sanctuary, nourishment, and care is fundamental for keeping Pygmy goats healthy and cheerful. A very much ventilated cover with insurance from outrageous weather patterns is vital. They expect admittance to clean water, quality feed, and a reasonable diet that incorporates grains and minerals. Standard veterinary care, immunizations and parasite control are additionally vital for their health.

Utilizes: While Pygmy goats are basically kept as pets and companions, they can likewise fill useful needs. Certain individuals raise them for their milk, fiber (on the off chance that they have angora hereditary qualities), or even as weed control in specific rural settings. Also, Pygmy goats are famous in petting zoos and instructive projects because of their manageable size and cordial attitude.

Breeding and Reproduction: Pygmy goats are productive raisers and can have numerous children in a solitary pregnancy. Pregnancy, otherwise called growth, ordinarily goes on around 145 to 153 days (around 5 months). Female Pygmy goats are known as does, and males are called bucks. Legitimate breeding management is fundamental to guarantee the health and well-being of both the mother and her offspring.

Pygmy goats are wonderful, conservative creatures that have caught the hearts of individuals around the world. Whether you're searching for an enchanting pet, a small scale farming endeavor, or an exceptional expansion to instructive projects, Pygmy goats can pursue a superb decision. Recollect that mindful care and consideration are vital to guaranteeing their cheerful and healthy lives.

CHOOSING AND CARING ON PYGMY GOATS

Pygmy goats are a famous decision for limited scope livestock proprietorship because of their conservative size, cordial nature, and generally low support necessities. Here is a manual for choosing and caring on pygmy goats:

Choosing Pygmy Goats:

1.   Breed Characteristics: Pygmy goats are a little variety, commonly gauging between 35 to 60 pounds and remaining around 16 to 23 inches tall at the shrinks. They have a solid form, short legs, and a conservative body.

2. Health and Personality: Pick goats that seem active, dynamic, and have a sparkling coat. Stay away from goats with indications of ailment, like runny eyes, nasal release, or coughing. Search for amicable and friendly goats that approach you without giving indications of hostility.

3. Age: While choosing pygmy goats, it's for the most part best to go for youngsters (child goats) or more youthful creatures. More seasoned goats might have laid out propensities that are more earnestly to change, and more youthful goats are simpler to train.

4. Sex: Conclude whether you need males (bucks), females (does), or a mix. Bucks can be more difficult to manage

because of their solid smell during breeding season, while does may require consideration during kidding (giving birth).

5.   Source: Purchase from respectable raisers who focus on the health and prosperity of their creatures. Request health records, immunization history, and ask about any past health issues.

Caring On Pygmy Goats:

1.   Housing: Give a solid and very much ventilated cover that shields the goats from harsh weather patterns, hunters, and drafts. The safe house ought to have clean sheet material like straw or wood shavings.

2. Fencing: Pygmy goats are light-footed climbers and jumpers. Utilize secure fencing that is somewhere around 4 to 5 feet high to forestall get away. Fencing ought to likewise have little holes to keep goats from stalling out.

3. Feeding: Offer a decent diet comprising of good-quality roughage, new water, and a goat-explicit pellet feed. You can likewise enhance their diet with new vegetables and natural products. Try not to feed them harmful plants like azaleas, rhododendrons, and yew.

4. Healthcare: Consistently trim hooves (each 6 to 8 weeks), give inoculations as suggested by a

veterinarian, and deworm the goats intermittently. Talk with a veterinarian for a health plan customized to your goats' necessities.

5. Social Association: Pygmy goats are social creatures and flourish in the organization of different goats. Keeping somewhere around two goats is prescribed to forestall dejection and fatigue.

6. Enrichment: Give toys, climbing designs, and things for mental excitement. Pygmy goats appreciate investigating their current circumstance and playing.

7. Breeding and Kidding: In the event that you intend to raise pygmy goats,

guarantee you have the information and assets to care for pregnant does and infant kids. Legitimate pre-birth care and help during kidding are critical.

8. Grooming: Routinely brush your goats to keep their coats perfect and liberated from parasites. Check their hooves, eyes, and ears for any indications of issues.

9. Training: Pygmy goats can be trained to answer fundamental orders, making handling and care simpler. Positive reinforcement strategies function admirably for training.

10. Local Guidelines: Really take a look at your neighborhood drafting and creature farming guidelines prior to

getting pygmy goats. A few regions might have limitations on livestock possession.

CHAPTER TWO

BREEDING AND REPRODUCTION

Breeding and reproduction of pygmy goats, as other goat breeds, include careful preparation and management to guarantee healthy offspring and an effective breeding system. Pygmy goats are a little variety that is fundamentally kept as pets, for show, and for meat creation. Here are a few central issues to consider while breeding and replicating pygmy goats:

1. Selecting Breeding Stock: Pick healthy pygmy goats with positive qualities like great conformity, appropriate size, and demeanor. Choosing creatures that satisfy breed guidelines and display solid genetics is

significant. Try not to raise goats with realized health issues or imperfections.

2. Age and Availability: Female pygmy goats, known as does, can typically be reared interestingly at around 7-8 months of age, yet it's recommended to hold on until they arrive at 1 year old to guarantee their physical and regenerative development. Male pygmy goats, known as bucks, can be utilized for breeding at around 7-8 months too.

3. Breeding Season: Pygmy goats are viewed as occasional reproducers, with their breeding season regularly happening in the fall. This is impacted by changes in day length. To expand

effective breeding, plan to acquaint the bucks with the does during this period.

4.   Estrus Cycle and Signs: The estrus pattern of a doe is approximately 18-21 days, with the doe being in heat for around 12-36 hours during this period. Indications of estrus might incorporate fretfulness, vocalization, an enlarged and blushed vulva, and expanded interest in the buck.

5.   Buck-to-Doe   Proportion: The prescribed buck-to-doe proportion is around 1:20, meaning one buck for each 20 does. Abusing a solitary buck can prompt   diminished   ripeness,   so exhausting them is significant not.

6.   Mating and Growth: During estrus, acquaint the buck with the doe(s) for mating. A solitary mating is generally adequate, however noticing different mating can assist with guaranteeing fruitful   treatment.   Pygmy   goat incubation endures roughly 145-153 days (close to 5 months).

7.   Pregnancy   and   Care: During pregnancy,   furnish   the   doe   with legitimate   sustenance,   including excellent feed and grain planned for pregnant goats. Normal veterinary care and immunizations are fundamental to guarantee a healthy pregnancy.

8.   Kidding: Pygmy goats by and large bring forth 1-3 children for every pregnancy. Set up a spotless, dry, and

safe kidding region with bedding and haven. Help the doe on the off chance that vital during work; however try not to mediate except if difficulties emerge. Screen the children intently after birth to guarantee they are nursing and flourishing.

9. Weaning: Children are normally weaned from their moms at around 8-12 weeks of age. Furnish them with a legitimate diet that incorporates feed, grain, and new water.

10. Record Keeping: Keep up with exhaustive records of breeding dates, incubation periods, and other applicable data for every goat. This helps track the health and breeding history of your group.

PYGMY GOAT BEHAVIOR AND SOCIAL DESIGN

Pygmy goats (Capra aegagrus hircus) are a little type of trained goats that are known for their well disposed and friendly nature. They are regularly kept as pets, for milk creation, and for weed control. Here is an outline of their behavior and social design:

1. Social Nature: Pygmy goats are exceptionally friendly creatures. They appreciate collaborating with people and different creatures, including different goats, and they flourish in a herd enviroment. They are in many cases kept in gatherings to fulfill their social requirements.

2. Hierarchy and Dominance hierarchy: In the same way as other crowd creatures, pygmy goats lay out a food chain inside their gathering. This progressive system assists with keeping everything under control and diminish struggle. Predominant goats regularly approach better assets like food and safe house, while subordinate goats might need to stand by.

3. Communication: Pygmy goats utilize different vocalizations and non-verbal communication to impart. They can cry out, snort, and even shout to communicate various feelings or requirements. They likewise use body act, head development, and tail position to convey their sentiments and goals.

4. Playful Behavior: Pygmy goats are known for their playful and inquisitive nature. They engage in exercises like running, hopping, and climbing, which assists them with fostering their muscles and coordination. Giving them open doors for play and investigation is significant for their prosperity.

5. Grooming: Prepping is a social behavior among pygmy goats. They frequently groom each other by licking, snacking, or scouring against one another. This behavior assists with fortifying social bonds inside the crowd and adds to keeping up with neatness.

6. Aggression and Struggle: While pygmy goats are by and large agreeable, clashes can emerge inside the crowd,

particularly during feeding times or while laying out predominance. Horned goats might engage in head-butting or different types of physical association during questions. Legitimate management and satisfactory room can assist with limiting forceful behavior.

7. Maternal Senses: Female pygmy goats (does) are mindful and defensive moms. They display solid maternal impulses, dealing with their young by preparing, nursing, and keeping them close for insurance.

8. Interspecies Communication: Pygmy goats can lay out certain associations with different creatures, including canines, chickens, and people. Their friendly nature permits them to

incorporate well into blended species settings, yet careful introductions and management are vital to guarantee everybody's security.

9. Enrichment and Mental Excitement: Giving pygmy goats mental and physical feeling is significant for their prosperity. Things like toys, stages, and designs to get on can assist with keeping them engaged and forestall fatigue.

CHAPTER THREE

TRAINING AND ADVANCEMENT FOR PYGMY GOATS

Training and improving pygmy goats can be a tomfoolery and compensating experience. Pygmy goats are smart and inquisitive creatures, and with appropriate training and advancement, you can assist with keeping them intellectually and physically invigorated. Here are a few methods for training and improving pygmy goats:

1. Socialization: Pygmy goats are social creatures, so it's vital to furnish them with chances to interface with different goats or many other cordial creatures. Social collaboration forestalls weariness and advances regular behaviors.

2. Positive reinforcement Training: Pygmy goats can be trained utilizing positive reinforcement procedures. Reward them with treats, like little bits of natural fruits or vegetables, when they show the ideal behavior. This could incorporate coming while called, strolling on a rope, or performing basic skills.

3. Fundamental Orders: Show your pygmy goats essential orders like "come," "remain," and "down." These orders can be helpful for overseeing them and protecting them.

4. Clicker Training: Clicker training is a famous strategy for training creatures. Utilize a clicker to check the ideal behavior, and afterward reward the goat

with a treat. This assists them with partner the snap sound with a positive result.

5. Leash Training: to take your pygmy goats for strolls, begin by acquainting them with a saddle and chain in a protected and controlled climate. Bit by bit get them used to wearing the outfit and chain prior to endeavoring to go for them for strolls outside.

6. Agility Training: Setting up a basic agility course can give mental and physical feeling to your goats. Use things like little obstacles, passages, and slopes to make a deterrent course that challenges them.

7. Improvement Exercises: Keep your pygmy goats intellectually engaged by giving advancement exercises. This can incorporate balancing up objects for them to examine, giving riddle feeders, or spreading food around their fenced in area to encourage regular rummaging behaviors.

8. Playtime and Toys: Offer an assortment of safe toys for your pygmy goats to play with. Things like enormous balls, ropes, and stages can keep them engaged and dynamic.

9. Grooming and Handling: Customary prepping and handling meetings can assist with building trust among you and your goats. Get them used to being

contacted, brushed, and analyzed to make veterinary care simpler.

10. Pivot and Fluctuate Improvement: To keep your goats from becoming exhausted, routinely turn and shift their enhancement exercises and toys. This keeps their current circumstance new and invigorating.

PYGMY GOAT HEALTH AND COMMON DISEASES

Pygmy goats are cute and famous pets that require appropriate care to guarantee their health and well-being. Very much like some other creature, they can be inclined to specific health issues. Here are some common pygmy goat health concerns and sicknesses, alongside tips for counteraction and therapy:

1. Parasites (Internal and external): Pygmy goats are powerless to both internal parasites like worms (e.g., gastrointestinal parasites) and outer parasites like lice and bugs. Normal deworming and legitimate cleanliness practices can assist with forestalling parasite pervasions.

2. Hoof Issues: Hoof issues like overgrowth, breaks, and abscesses can happen in pygmy goats. Customary foot managing and support are fundamental to forestall these issues. Counsel a veterinarian or an accomplished goat manager for direction on legitimate foot care.

3. Respiratory Contaminations: Goats, including pygmy goats, can foster respiratory diseases because of unfortunate ventilation, cold and soggy circumstances, or openness to other debilitated creatures. Proper housing and management can assist with lessening the risk of respiratory issues.

4. Bloat: Bloat is a condition where gas gathers in the goat's stomach, making distress and possibly carrying on with an existence compromising circumstance. Feeding top notch forage, keeping away from abrupt diet changes, and giving admittance to new, clean water can assist with forestalling bloat.

5. Urinary Calculi: Male pygmy goats are more inclined to urinary calculi

(bladder stones) because of their special urinary life systems. Giving a legitimate calcium-to-phosphorus proportion in their diet, alongside a lot of water and exercise, can assist with forestalling urinary calculi.

6. Pneumonia: Pneumonia can be brought about by bacterial or viral contaminations. Great ventilation, clean everyday environments, and limiting pressure can decrease the risk of pneumonia. Inoculations against normal respiratory microbes can likewise help.

7. External Wounds: Pygmy goats can be interested and playful, now and then prompting unintentional wounds. Giving a completely safe climate can assist with forestalling these episodes.

8.   Malnutrition: Ill-advised feeding can prompt lack of healthy sustenance, heftiness, or other dietary-related issues. Guarantee your goats approach adjusted nourishment, including great quality roughage, legitimate mineral supplementation, and suitable commercial goat feed.

9.   Reproductive Issues: Female pygmy goats might encounter entanglements during pregnancy or birthing. Standard veterinary care and checking during pregnancy are urgent to guarantee healthy pregnancies and conveyances.

10.   Heat Pressure: Pygmy goats are delicate to warm and can experience the ill effects of intensity stress during

blistering climate. Give conceal, appropriate ventilation, and admittance to spotless, cool water to assist them with remaining agreeable.

11. Foot Decay: Foot decay is an infectious bacterial disease that influences the hooves. Keep up with perfect and dry day to day environments to limit the risk of foot decay. Brief treatment with veterinary care is significant in the event that foot decay is thought.

CHAPTER FOUR

PREVENTIVE HEALTH MEASURES

Pygmy goats, similar to all creatures, benefit from legitimate preventive health measures to guarantee their health and life span. Here are a few significant advances you can take to keep up with the health of your pygmy goats:

1. Routine Veterinary Care: Lay out a relationship with an accomplished veterinarian with goats, ideally one who spends significant time in little ruminants or livestock. Plan ordinary check-ups for your pygmy goats to early screen their health and catch any expected issues.

2.   Vaccinations: Work with your vet to foster an inoculation plan suitable for your district. Normal immunizations for goats might incorporate security against sicknesses like lockjaw, Clostridium perfringens (gorging illness), and other common infections in your space.

3.   Parasite Control: Goats are powerless to internal parasites like worms, as well as outer parasites like lice and vermin. Foster a deworming plan for conference with your vet to monitor parasites. Turn fields and practice great sterilization to limit parasite openness.

4.   Nutrition and Diet: Give a reasonable and healthfully sufficient diet for your pygmy goats. Their diet ought

to incorporate excellent roughage, new water, and potentially goat-explicit pelleted feed. Abstain from overfeeding, as corpulence can prompt health issues.

5. Clean Housing: Guarantee that your pygmy goats approach perfect and dry haven. Appropriate housing can safeguard them from outrageous atmospheric conditions and diminish the risk of respiratory issues.

6. Hoof Care: Consistently trim your goats' hooves to forestall abundance and inconvenience. Dismissed hooves can prompt faltering and other health issues.

7. Dental Health: Screen your goats' dental health and give fitting materials to them to bite on. Dental issues can

influence their capacity to appropriately eat and process food.

8. Hygiene: Practice great cleanliness and sterilization in the goat region. Clean water and feeding regions routinely to forestall the spread of sickness.

9. Quarantine and Biosecurity: On the off chance that you acquaint new goats with your crowd, quarantine them for a while prior to incorporating them. This forestalls the spread of expected illnesses to your current goats.

10. Exercise and Enhancement: Permit your pygmy goats to have normal activity and admittance to an invigorating climate. Advancement

exercises can advance mental and physical prosperity.

11. Observation: Invest energy noticing your pygmy goats every day. This permits you to rapidly see any progressions in behavior, hunger, or health and address potential issues immediately.

12. Stress Management: Limit stressors for your goats, as stress can debilitate their invulnerable framework and make them more powerless to sicknesses. Stay away from unexpected changes in their current circumstance or schedule.

RECOGNIZING INDICATIONS OF SICKNESS

Recognizing indications of sickness in pygmy goats is pivotal for keeping up with their health and well-being. Pygmy goats are helpless to an assortment of health issues, very much like some other creature. Here are typical indications of disease to keep an eye out for:

1.   Changes in Behavior: In the event that a typically dynamic and playful pygmy goat becomes dormant, withdrawn, or disconnected from the crowd, it very well may be an indication of disease.

2.   Lack of Appetite: An unexpected lessening in hunger or refusal to eat can show a health issue. Watch out for their

dietary patterns and screen their water intake.

3. Weight Misfortune: In the event that you notice a critical deficiency of weight in a brief period, it could be an indication of a fundamental health issue.

4. Dull Coat: A healthy pygmy goat ought to have a sparkly and smooth coat. A dull or unkempt coat could be an indication of sickness or unfortunate nourishment.

5. Coughing and Sniffling: Respiratory issues like coughing, wheezing, nasal release, or toiled breathing could be demonstrative of diseases or other respiratory issues.

6. Diarrhea or Clogging: Irregularities in defecations can be an indication of digestive issues, contaminations, or parasites.

7. Eye or Nose Release: Exorbitant release from the eyes or nose, particularly on the off chance that it's thick, shaded, or noxious, could demonstrate disease.

8. Lameness or Trouble Strolling: On the off chance that a pygmy goat is limping, leaning toward one leg, or experiencing issues strolling, it very well may be because of injury, disease, or joint issues.

9. Swelling or Irregularities: Any strange knots, knocks, or expanding on

the body ought to be inspected by a veterinarian.

10. Behavioral Changes: Hostility, extreme head squeezing, surrounding, or other strange behaviors might propose neurological issues.

11. Teeth Crushing or Slobbering: These signs could demonstrate dental issues or torment.

12. Fever: A raised internal heat level can be a sign of a contamination or other basic issue. Typical goat internal heat level reaches from 101.5°F to 104.5°F (38.6°C to 40.3°C).

13. Dehydration: Check for indented eyes, dry mouth, and tacky gums. Drying

out can be a serious concern, particularly in blistering climate.

14. Scratching and Scouring: Unreasonable scratching or scouring against surfaces could be an indication of skin bothering, parasites, or sensitivities.

CHAPTER FIVE

PYGMY GOATS IN SUSTAINABLE AGRICULTURE

Pygmy goats can play a role in sustainable farming through different ways. These little, tough goats have specific characteristics that make them appropriate for sustainable cultivating rehearses. Here are a few manners by which pygmy goats can add to practical farming:

1. Weed Control: Pygmy goats are amazing slow eaters and can assist with controlling weeds and undergrowth in pastures and different regions. Rather than utilizing synthetic herbicides or mechanical strategies, goats can be utilized as regular weed control agents,

diminishing the requirement for earth destructive practices.

2. Land Management: Goats are known for their capacity to clear and manage vegetation in regions that are challenging for apparatus to get to. They can assist with clearing congested fields, brush, and bushes, making land more usable for agribusiness or different purposes.

3. Manure Creation: Goat excrement is a significant wellspring of natural compost. It very well may be treated the soil and used to further develop soil fruitfulness, advancing healthy plant development without depending on engineered manures.

4. Diversification: Integrating pygmy goats into a differentiated cultivating framework can upgrade generally ranch versatility. By having different kinds of livestock and yields, ranchers can lessen the dangers related with monoculture and be more ready to adjust to evolving conditions.

5. Educational Opportunities: Pygmy goats can act as instructive apparatuses, helping bring issues to light about reasonable horticulture among kids and grown-ups. Ranchers can have studios, ranch visits, and different occasions to exhibit the advantages of integrating goats into their cultivating rehearse.

6. Local Food Creation: Pygmy goats can give a wellspring of privately

delivered meat and dairy items, adding to the advancement of neighborhood and feasible food frameworks. Limited scope goat cultivating can likewise uphold nearby economies and decrease the carbon impression related with moving food significant distances.

7. Low Information Necessities: Pygmy goats are moderately simple to care for and have lower feed prerequisites contrasted with bigger livestock. They can blossom with forage, peruse, and other regular vegetation, diminishing the requirement for serious feed inputs.

8. Small-Scale Cultivating: Pygmy goats are appropriate for limited scope and lawn cultivating tasks. They require

less space contrasted with bigger livestock, making them available for people with restricted land assets.

9. Fiber Creation: While not quite so normal as in bigger goat breeds, pygmy goats can likewise deliver fiber, like mohair or cashmere. This can turn out extra revenue streams for ranchers who focus on practical fiber creation.

10. Genetic Variety: Raising pygmy goats adds to the safeguarding of hereditary variety in livestock populaces, which is significant for keeping up with versatile and versatile creatures despite changing ecological circumstances.

PYGMY GOAT BREEDING FOR BEIGNNERS

Breeding pygmy goats can be a fulfilling and pleasant experience, yet it requires careful preparation, information, and obligation to the prosperity of the creatures. Here are a few stages and tips for beginners keen on pygmy goat breeding:

1.   Educate Yourself: Before you begin breeding pygmy goats, it's fundamental to teach yourself about their essential necessities, behavior, health care, and breeding practices. Assets like books, online gatherings, and nearby rural augmentation workplaces can give important data.

2.   Select Healthy and Quality Goats: Pick breeding stock that is healthy, all around organized, and adjusts to raise guidelines. Search for pygmy goats with great compliance, solid hereditary qualities, and advantageous attributes like size, variety, and personality. It's smart to source your goats from respectable reproducers to guarantee their quality.

3.   Plan Your Breeding System: Decide your objectives for breeding. Is it true or not that you are breeding for pets, show creatures, or milk creation? Characterize your breeding targets and select goats that line up with those objectives.

4.   Age and Development: Female pygmy goats, known as does, ought to be

somewhere around 8 to 10 months old prior to breeding interestingly. Guys, or bucks, can be prepared to raise as soon as 3 to 4 months old, however it's not unexpected better to hold on until they are around 6 to 8 months old to guarantee their development.

5. Breeding Season: Pygmy goats are occasional reproducers, with their breeding season commonly happening in the fall. Bucks become more dynamic and intrigued by does during this time. Nonetheless, it's fundamental to guarantee that your goats are healthy and condition prior to breeding.

6. Health Care: Prior to breeding, ensure your goats are state-of-the-art on immunizations, deworming, and

generally health care. A veterinarian experienced with goats can direct you through this interaction.

7. Housing and Space: Give appropriate lodging and space to your goats. They need cover from harsh weather patterns, satisfactory room to move around, and a spotless climate. Sufficient fencing is vital to forestall get away and safeguard the goats from hunters.

8. Nutrition: Legitimate sustenance is fundamental for fruitful breeding and healthy children (child goats). Furnish your goats with a reasonable diet of good-quality roughage, new water, and proper goat feed. Pregnant and nursing

wills have expanded healthful requirements.

9. Mating Cycle: Acquaint the buck with the pens' instead of the reverse way around. Watch out for their associations, and eliminate the buck assuming that hostility turns into an issue. Bucks might require a lead goat to follow or a secret doe to invigorate interest.

10. Pregnancy and Birth: The growth time frame for pygmy goats is around 145 to 155 days (roughly 5 months). Furnish the pregnant doe with legitimate care and sustenance all through her pregnancy. Set up a perfect, calm region for kidding (conceiving an

offspring), and screen the interaction intently.

11. Kid Care: When the children are conceived, guarantee they get colostrum (the first milk rich in quite a while) from their mom. Give a warm and clean climate for the children to flourish. Bottle feeding may be fundamental assuming that the mother can't care for them satisfactorily.

12. Record Keeping: Keep up with precise records of breeding dates, birth dates, health care, inoculations, and other significant data. This will assist you with following the headway of your breeding system and settle on informed choices.

CHAPTER SIX

PYGMY GOATS AS PETS: CONTEMPLATIONS AND CARE

Pygmy goats can make awesome and engaging pets, yet they additionally require appropriate care and thought. Here are a few significant focuses to know whether you're thinking about embracing pygmy goats as pets:

1.   Space and Shelter: Pygmy goats need sufficient room to wander, brush, and play. A closed in region is fundamental for guard them from hunters. Give a strong haven that shields them from cruel weather patterns, like downpour, cold, and over the top intensity.

2.   Social Creatures: Pygmy goats are profoundly friendly animals and flourish in the organization of different goats. It's prescribed to have somewhere around two goats to forestall dejection and give friendship.

3.   Feeding and Nourishment: A fair diet is essential for pygmy goats' health. Give excellent roughage, new water, and a specific goat feed to meet their nourishing necessities. Try not to take feed them human food or plants that may be poisonous to them.

4.   Veterinary Care: Normal health check-ups and inoculations are critical to keep up with the prosperity of your pygmy goats. Lay out a relationship with

a veterinarian experienced in treating goats.

5. Hoof Care: Pygmy goats' hooves need customary managing to forestall abundance and related health issues. Figure out how to manage hooves appropriately or enlist an expert if necessary.

6. Exercise and Advancement: Pygmy goats are dynamic and playful creatures. Give them potential open doors for practice and mental excitement, like climbing structures and toys.

7. Grooming: Standard prepping assists keep pygmy goats with cleaning and agreeable. Brush their coats to

forestall matting and check for any indications of parasites.

8. Waste Management: Legitimate waste management is urgent. Routinely spotless their living region to forestall the development of waste and limit the risk of illness.

9. Zoning and Guidelines: Actually take a look at neighborhood drafting regulations and guidelines prior to keeping pygmy goats as pets. A few regions might have limitations on livestock possession.

10. Training and Handling: Begin training and handling your pygmy goats since early on to guarantee they are agreeable around people. This will make

veterinary visits and generally speaking care simpler.

11. Breeding Contemplations: On the off chance that you intend to raise pygmy goats, be ready for the obligations of breeding and bringing up kids. Overpopulation can turn into an issue on the off chance that goats are not dependably reared and managed.

12. Behavioral Qualities: Pygmy goats have unmistakable behaviors and characters. They can be wicked and inquisitive, so be ready for their playful shenanigans.

13. Time Responsibility: Keeping pygmy goats demands a huge time

responsibility. They need day to day care, consideration, and observing.

14. Longevity: Pygmy goats have a life expectancy of around 10-15 years or more with legitimate care. Think about the drawn out responsibility prior to bringing them into your home.

PYGMY GOAT MILK AND DAIRY CREATION

Pygmy goats are a little variety of homegrown goats that are fundamentally saved for fancy and side interest purposes. While they in all actuality do create milk, their milk yield is altogether lower contrasted with bigger dairy goat breeds like Nubians or Saanens. Subsequently, pygmy goats are not normally raised for business dairy creation, but rather a few limited scope ranchers and homesteaders might decide to use their milk for individual use.

Here are a few central issues about pygmy goat milk and dairy creation:

1.   Milk Yield: Pygmy goats produce considerably less milk contrasted with bigger dairy goat breeds. On average, they might deliver around 1 to 2 quarts of milk each day, while bigger dairy goat breeds can create 2 to 4 times that sum.

2.   Milk Arrangement: Pygmy goat milk is for the most part comparable in organization to drain from other goat breeds, containing higher fat substance than cow's milk. It very well may be

utilized to make cheddar, yogurt, and other dairy items.

3.   Diet and Sustenance: To guarantee great milk quality, pygmy goats require a decent and nutritious diet. Their diet ought to incorporate excellent feed, grains, new water, and admittance to minerals and nutrients.

4.   Milking Everyday practice: On the off chance that you intend to drain pygmy goats, it's vital to lay out a customary draining daily schedule. Draining ought to be done in a perfect and clean climate to forestall defilement of the milk.

5.   Hygiene and Health: Appropriate cleanliness rehearses are fundamental to

keep up with the health of the goats and the nature of their milk. Ordinary health checks, inoculations, and parasite control are significant parts of goat care.

6.   Use of Milk: The milk from pygmy goats can be utilized to make different dairy items, including cheddar, yogurt, and cleanser. In any case, because of their lower milk yield, these items are commonly delivered on a limited scale for individual utilization or nearby deals.

7.   Breeding and Hereditary qualities: Assuming that you're keen on pygmy goat milk creation, it's critical to choose breeding stock with great milk lines to amplify milk yield. In any case, remember that even with specific

breeding, pygmy goats won't deliver milk in that frame of mind to bigger dairy breeds.

8. Regulations: Assuming you intend to sell any dairy items from your pygmy goats, make a point to explore and comply to any nearby guidelines with respect to drain creation, handling, and deals.

CHAPTER SEVEN

PYGMY GOAT GENETICS AND COLORS VARIATIATIONS

Pygmy goats are a little variety of homegrown goats that started in West Africa. They are known for their conservative size, amicable demeanor, and versatility to different conditions. With regards to their genetics and color varieties, there are a couple of central issues to consider:

Genetics Of Pygmy Goats:

1. Basic Genetics: Pygmy goat hereditary qualities follow similar standards as other homegrown goats. They acquire qualities from their folks as qualities.

2.   Inheritance: The legacy of qualities is constrained by sets of qualities, where each parent contributes one quality to the pair. A few characteristics are prevailing (communicated when just a single duplicate is available) and some are passive (communicated just when two duplicates are available).

3.   Color and Coat Genetics: The variety and coat pattern of Pygmy goats are impacted by various qualities. A portion of the fundamental variety qualities incorporate Agouti (A), Expansion (E), and Black (B). Various mixes of these qualities bring about the different variety designs found in Pygmy goats.

Color Variations:

1. Agouti: Agouti alludes to the dissemination of varieties on the goat's body. Pygmy goats can display a scope of agouti designs, including strong varieties, belted designs, and different mixes of varieties on their body.

2. Extension Quality: The Expansion quality decides if a goat has a dark coat or a red coat. Goats with the prevailing expansion quality (EE or Ee) will have a dark coat, while goats with two latent augmentation qualities (ee) will have a red coat.

3. Black and Brown: The Black quality (B) and Brown colored quality (b) decide if dark shade will be created. At the

point when a goat has two dark qualities (BB), it produces dark shade. At the point when it has two brown colored qualities (bb), it produces brown colored shade. A goat with one of every (Bb) will for the most part seem dark however can convey the brown colored quality.

4.   Pattern Varieties: Pygmy goats can likewise display different patterns, including strong, agouti, iced (roaning), and different blends of these patterns.

5.   White Markings: Some Pygmy goats might have white markings all over, legs, and body. These markings are impacted by independent qualities.

PYGMY GOAT CARE IN VARIOUS ENVIRONMENTS

Pygmy goats are a little and maybe solid variety that can adjust to different environments, yet their care prerequisites ought to be changed in light of the particular states of the environment they are kept in. Here are a few basic principles for really focusing on pygmy goats in various environments:

1.   Cold Environments:

a.   Shelter: Give a very much protected and without draft cover for your pygmy goats to safeguard them from brutal breezes and cold temperatures. The safe house ought to be dry and all around ventilated.

b. Bedding: Utilize straw or feed bedding to keep the goats warm and off the virus ground. Consistently change the sheet material to keep up with neatness and warmth.

c. Water: Guarantee admittance to new, thawed water consistently. Utilize warmed water pails or a warmed water supply to forestall freezing.

d. Nutrition: Increment their feed during colder months to assist them with producing more body heat. Great roughage and goat feed with suitable supplements are significant.

e. Health: Check for frostbite on their ears, udders, and hooves. Give normal health checks and admittance to veterinary care.

2.   Hot and Dry Environments:

a.   Shade: Give adequate shade to safeguard pygmy goats from direct daylight. Heat pressure is a worry, so ensure they have a concealed region over the course of the day.

b.   Water: Keep them all around hydrated by giving spotless, cool water. Ensure water sources are effectively open and routinely renewed.

c.   Nutrition: Change their diet in light of intensity conditions. Give admittance to new, excellent forage, and consider adding electrolyte supplements during outrageous intensity to forestall parchedness.

d. Ventilation: Guarantee great wind stream in their sanctuary to forestall heat development. Legitimate ventilation manages their internal heat level.

e. Hoof Care: Trim their hooves routinely to forestall excess and distress, which can be exacerbated by hot and dry circumstances.

3. Humid Environments:

a. Shelter: Give a sanctuary that safeguards pygmy goats from downpour and mugginess. Guarantee great ventilation to forestall the development of shape and mold.

b.   Health Management: Screen for indications of skin issues, for example, parasitic contaminations, which can flourish in sticky conditions. Customary grooming and dry sheet material can assist with forestalling these issues.

c.   Nutrition: Be wary about feed storage to forestall shape development. Consider changing their diet to address the particular difficulties of a muggy environment.

d.   Water: Guarantee that water compartments are cleaned habitually to forestall green growth development and defilement.

CONCLUSION

Pygmy goats are a little and famous variety of trained goats known for their conservative size, well disposed characters, and various variety designs. They have gained critical ubiquity as pets, partners, and, surprisingly, now and again, as livestock for milk and meat creation. All in all, Pygmy goats offer a few advantages and contemplations:

Advantages:

1.   Size: Pygmy goats are little in size, making them reasonable for more modest properties and lawn arrangements.

2.   Personality: They are by and large amicable, inquisitive, and social

creatures, making them incredible mates and pets.

3. Low Support: Pygmy goats require less space and feed contrasted with bigger goat breeds, making them more straightforward to care for.

4. Milk and Meat: While not essential wellsprings of milk or meat creation, Pygmy goats can in any case give a modest quantity of milk and meat for individual utilization.

5. Land Management: They can assist with controlling vegetation and weeds in a controlled brushing climate.

Contemplations:

1.　Space: Despite the fact that they require less space than bigger varieties, Pygmy goats actually need satisfactory space for exercise and touching.

2.　Social Necessities: Pygmy goats are social creatures and flourish in the organization of different goats. It is prescribed to Keep somewhere around two goats.

3.　Health Care: Standard health care and upkeep, including inoculations and foot managing, are important to keep them healthy.

4.　Zoning Guidelines: Actually take a look at nearby drafting guidelines and limitations prior to keeping Pygmy goats, as certain areas might have explicit principles in regards to livestock proprietorship.

5. Longevity: Pygmy goats have a life expectancy of around 10 to 15 years, requiring a drawn out responsibility.

Basically, Pygmy goats can be brilliant increments to families or little ranches, giving friendship, diversion, and restricted assets like milk and meat. Notwithstanding, planned proprietors ought to be ready to give legitimate care, consideration, and reasonable everyday environments for these enchanting creatures.

THE END

Printed in Great Britain
by Amazon

41020742R00046